Success in Football

*Steve Perryman, Captain of
Tottenham Hotspur, being
presented with the F.A. Cup
by H.R.H. Princess Michael
of Kent at the end of the
100th Cup Final*

Photo by Bob Thomas

Success in

Football

MIKE SMITH

F.A. Staff Coach
formerly Manager, Hull City A.F.C.
and Manager and Director of Coaching,
The Football Association of Wales

With a Foreword by
ALLEN WADE
formerly Director of Coaching,
The Football Association

JOHN MURRAY

Success Sportsbooks

Athletics
Football
Golf
Netball
Rugby
Swimming
Volleyball
Weight Training

© Michael J. Smith 1973, 1978, 1981, 1982, 1983
First published 1973
Second edition 1978
Third edition 1982
Reprinted 1983

Printed in Hong Kong
0 7195 3900 5

CONTENTS

FOREWORD

Many books have been written about footballers; a few have even been written *by* footballers, but very few indeed have been written *about* football by coaches, the men whose business it is to guide and influence the development of players at all levels at which the game is played.

Football coaches are practical men and coaching is a practical matter which involves the effective transference of experience, knowledge and understanding, from one person to another. To put over football knowledge and experience in a book is a difficult exercise indeed, but this book, written by a man who has had great practical experience as a player, as Manager of Hull City and as Director of Coaching and Manager to the Welsh international teams, has succeeded where a large number have failed.

Football is a simple game often complicated, unfortunately, by people. Michael Smith has succeeded in presenting his valuable football ideas in a simple and uncomplicated way. His book will be a most welcome addition to the growing store of international football wisdom. I wish that I had written it.

ALLEN WADE
formerly Director of Coaching
The Football Association

Mike Smith
coaching players
(by courtesy o
the Western Mai

6

ACKNOWLEDGMENTS

I am indebted to the skill and co-operation of Bob Hewitt of North Wales News Pictures. You will be able to judge his ability for yourself by the series of excellent photographs of Welsh International players in this book. The four players – goalkeeper Brian Lloyd, defender Mickey Evans, defender Gareth Davis and forward Arfon Griffiths – have fully demonstrated their ample skills and to each of them I am most grateful. I am grateful to the Board of Directors, John Neal, former Manager, and the staff of Wrexham A.F.C. who have so willingly co-operated in the preparation of this book. I would also like to thank Dunlop Limited for their help and encouragement.

Many of the action shots of top stars performing specific skills were taken by Bob Thomas Sports Photography to whom I must express thanks. Others were by Sport & General Photographic Agency and the *Liverpool Daily Post and Echo Limited*. The photograph of Terry Yorath (page 59) was supplied by the *Coventry Evening Telegraph*, those of Brian Flynn (page 54) and Leighton James (page 65) by Mark Leech, and John Toshack (page 75) by Doug Mortimer.

Photographs provide a visual guide to performance. The superb skills of top stars are imitated by young players. It is the top international players who set the pattern for every aspiring young player. I am pleased and privileged to portray each star featured. I have selected them because I admire their skill and the way they play the game.   M.S.

INTRODUCTION

Football thrives on success. There is more written about promotion than relegation, more about cup winners than cup losers. Throughout the many leagues, from primary schools right through to the Football League, it is the competitive framework that sets the scene season after season. The few supreme honours are fought for to the end. Success boosts crowds, excites supporters, gives dreams of greatness to players and managers. Failure not only means disappointment; in the top flight it means the sack.

In my experience in dealing with young players, there is no substitute for skill. Skill is the one ingredient that cannot be given – it is a gift. My job in coaching – and the job of all teachers and coaches – is to recognise skill. We can help and improve on a player's techniques, but only he can learn to apply those techniques to his own natural skills. The distinction between skill and technique is important. *Technique* is the basic physical mastery of kicking, heading, tackling, etc. *Skill* is the application of these techniques against opponents. For instance two players can kick a ball to each other for ever, and until somebody tries to dispossess them they learn nothing. But success, even to the most gifted, never comes easily. Hard work, match play, hard work and more hard work is the single formula for success.

This book examines, position by position, the various techniques and skills required by every good player. It endeavours to be a logical guide to the main priorities of each position and offers young players the opportunity of self-examination by comparing their skills and thoughts on the game with mine.

Football is a game which revolves around decisions. Simple when you know how, but because of the number of co-operating players and opposing players, the simplicity is always in the eyes of the onlooker. In the good team, players will harness together the right decisions at the right time, and will make decisions for each other. In the bad team, confusion goes from bad to worse because decisions are so difficult to make that the conflict in the players' minds produces the wrong ones.

In Part 1 I have looked at basic techniques and skills, and in Part 2 I have examined the application of these skills to the game. The application of skills can only be put into effect when a player has a complete understanding of the *principles of play*. The terms used are collective and allow players freedom to express themselves and to understand each other. For instance if you are a highly talented 'Trevor Francis' type of player it would be futile for the team to rely on you always to go it alone and score. But, if the other forwards play a full part, when it really *is* possible for you to attack alone, the surprise element can often be enough to make you outstandingly successful. In other words each player should be allowed free expression of his individual talent within the full understanding of the underlying principles.

The principles of play are far more important than systems of play. There is so much confusion when we play numbers, especially with young players, because every team, even under eleven, identifies itself strongly with top teams and may start to play with eight players back and play 1–4–4–2. I heard of a manager's son of seven who came home from playing football for his school with a very long face. 'What's the matter, lad? Did you lose? 'No,' replied the boy. 'We won 4–0, but I never had a kick. I was a *sweeper* in a 1–4–2–4.' This, to me, is what teachers and coaches must fight against. Success is one thing, but success which does not allow the fullest scope to each individual is something quite different – and wrong. It is essential that every player should be given the chance to develop according to his interests and abilities. A boy should play in many positions before he finds out where he can play best.

In Part 3 I have examined restarts. Working out how to score from corners, free kicks and throw-ins gives all the team complete involvement. Everyone will have jobs to do and there is great satisfaction in scoring from these set plays.

Part 4 deals briefly with fitness. If you are not fit, you can't play well. But there are so many approaches to keeping fit that it is outside the scope of this book to go into them in detail. Coaches and teachers will give specific guidance here . . . I can merely offer advice and point in the right direction.

In showing photographs to illustrate certain possibilities of passing the ball in Parts 1 and 2, Bob Hewitt has shown remarkable ability with a wide-angled lens on his camera – a tip picked up from Zagallo, the ex-manager of the Brazilian team that won the 1970 World Cup and now manager of Kuwait. Zagallo had a press friend who took hundreds of wide-angled lens photographs in the 1968 match between West Germany and Brazil. Zagallo was then able to show the tactical deployment, both good and bad, of the Brazilian team, and to make highly individual players understand their collective responsibilities. I sincerely hope that as each one of you reads this book you will come to a better understanding of yourself as a player – both as an individual and as part of a team.   M.S.

PART 1   *INDIVIDUAL TECHNIQUES AND SKILLS*

I said in the introduction that principles of play are more important than systems of play. This is so, but it is important to realise that modern football has made adjustments over the past twenty years and offers slightly different terms to describe positions from those formerly used. On the chart that follows I have shown the name of each position on the field, and these positions are the same for every team, although different teams deploy their men in different ways. Liverpool, for instance, is a team which has shown a consistency of performance that can only be maintained by a high degree of skill in each individual player. The team's formation usually starts as 1–4–3–3, but can fluctuate, depending on the game. Here it is.

	1 Bruce Grobbelaar *goalkeeper*	
2 Phil Neal *right back*	6 Alan Hansen *sweeper*	3 Alan Kennedy *left back*
	4 Phil Thompson *centre back*	
10 Terry McDermott *midfield*	11 Graham Souness *midfield*	5 Ray Kennedy *midfield*
7 Kenny Dalglish *striker*	8 Sammy Lee *midfield*	9 David Johnson *winger*

In Chapters 1–8 I analyse the play for each specific position: Chapter 1, goalkeepers, like the agile Ray Clemence or Joe Corrigan. Chapter 2, full backs, like Kenny Sansom or Phil Neal, showing their techniques, and indeed an overlap where the full back moves past his forwards into an advanced position. Chapter 3, centre backs such as Phil Thompson, Gordon McQueen or Dave Watson. Chapter 4, defensive wing half, sweeper or centre back, such as Bryan Robson, Alan Hansen or Russell

Osman, who play behind the centre half and the full backs, thus 'sweeping' across the field as the last defender. These defenders are shown to *intercept* (see pages 23 and 36) the ball when possible, *jockey* or *contain* (see pages 23 and 36) their opponent when it is not and *tackle* (see page 25) firmly the moment they feel they can. Chapter 5, midfield play.

In order to achieve the heights of success that Liverpool has, a lot depends on the amount and quality of play produced in midfield. This work is divided between winning the ball by closing down on opponents, and restricting their play (see pages 58–62), but the quality of control and pass are the true elements of success. In Chapter 6 I examine the defensive qualities of midfield play – Terry Yorath is always so quick to close in on opponents and contain them. Chapter 7, wing play. Few people who saw him play will forget the magic of George Best at his finest. But players such as Leighton James, Peter Barnes and John Robertson all have the fabulous qualities of pace and skill to beat their opponents and cross the ball accurately. Phil Neal is always prepared to push forward down the right flank and to cross the ball like those I have just mentioned. Chapter 8, strikers. The outstanding heading ability of John Toshack, coupled with the speed, skill and bravery of Kevin Keegan were once a feature of Liverpool's play. Now everybody is watching the success of Souness, Dalglish and McDermott. The whole side is geared to scoring goals right up to the final whistle, which is, after all, what the game is all about.

1 Goalkeeping

The goalkeepers are the 'poor relations' in the team. They get the least attention and very little constructive help. But the goalkeeper's role is one of the most important in the game, and if you are to become a good one, you must really work hard on your own to reach the stage where your decisions and reactions are instinctive.

1. 80 per cent of your work is 'fielding' the ball by acting rather like a sweeper behind the defence and catching and gathering balls played through the defence.

2. Always get your body behind the ball and keep your eyes on it.

3. You must always attack high balls to catch them as early as possible. (Then bring the ball straight to the chest.)

4. To deal with crosses you must position yourself within safety margins related to the near and far posts. Never expose either post.

5. You must continually adjust your position to adequately cover your goal. In other words you continually offer as little as possible of the goal to oncoming forwards.

6. When diving be sideways on, chest behind the ball, so that maximum vision will be maintained.

7. When diving horizontally off the ground make sure that you get your top hand to the ball and catch it, otherwise you tend to palm out shots to oncoming forwards.

8. It is important to develop the techniques of throwing the ball hard and straight; and kicking either a dead ball, or one from the hand, accurately and long. Distribution of the ball is a vital part of goalkeeping.

9. The goalkeeper must possess great courage, confidence, agility and strength. He must develop the ability to *concentrate totally* in order to produce the correct decisions after long periods of inactivity.

10. *There is no room for error. Examine the skill sequences and become expert at them all.*

SUCCESS
Ray Clemence
(Tottenham Hotspur and England)

Amazing reaction save by Jimmy Rimmer (Aston Villa) in stopping a close-range shot from Wallace (Coventry City).

SHOT SAVING: DIVING

1. Keep your feet close together for speed of movement.

2. Get your chest behind or close to the ball.

3. Get both hands round the ball and catch. To parry only offers an easy chance to oncoming forwards.

4. Always be sideways on in order to see the ball as long as possible.

5. Make sure you understand your angles relative to the shot and your posts.

HIGH CROSSES: CATCHING

1. Attack the ball to catch it as early as possible.

2. Only leave your line if you are sure of getting the ball.

3. Do not over-commit yourself beyond the near post for fear of exposing your far post. Also make sure that a cross cannot squeeze into the nearside.

4. Always protect yourself.

Peter Shilton (Nottingham Forest and England) catches a driven cross. Same principles.

Photos by Bob Thomas

14

(a) Crouch.
(b) Body weight forward onto the balls of your feet for correct balance.

(a) Take off.
(b) Effort to get horizontal.
(c) Top hand onto ball to catch.

(a) Point of contact.
(b) Both hands on ball catching it.
(c) Eye on ball.
(d) Body sideways on.

Initial position for a cross.

Close-up of hands behind the ball.

Pick out line of cross and attack the ball to catch it as early as possible.

15

DIVING AT FEET

1. Stay on your line when the forward is under close challenge from a defender.

2. When you go, go *fast*. Gather yourself for a shot, or a change of the forward's path.

3. Make a big obstacle, but offer little of the goal to shoot at.

4. When you decide to go — go down fast spreading your body as wide as possible across the ball.

5. Protect your head with your top arm.

6. As soon as you have it, curl up to the ball.

John Jackson (Millwall) diving at the feet of Mike Channon (Southampton and England).

Peter Shilton (Nottingham Forest and England) punching clear.

Jean Castadena (St. Etienne). pushing over the bar.

16

Photos by Bob Thomas

Note how little of the goal there is to shoot at.

Goalkeeper diving at feet.

PUNCHING CLEAR

You only punch when, having moved for the ball, players get in the way. Then you must force through them to make contact. To gain extra height use just one hand. If you can get two fists to it you might catch. Punch through the ball.

TURNING OVER THE BAR: FROM THE LEFT, AND FROM THE RIGHT

When the ball is curling dangerously under the bar — it is safer to turn it over the bar because quite often the challenge is from behind you. Use whichever hand you feel happier with. Hit towards the flight of ball.

KICKING A DEAD BALL

(a) Goalkeepers must learn to kick farther than any other players.

(b) Lengthen your last stride to the ball to give a longer swing.

(c) Hit through the ball with a straight leg, and follow right through.

(d) Hit for distance rather than height.

KICKING FROM THE HAND

(a) Wait until the ball nears the ground and kick with a straight leg.

(b) This will help give you distance rather than height.

Pat Jennings (Arsenal and N. Ireland)

18

THROWING THE BALL OUT

(a) Change the flank by a hard low throw wide and square to the full back.

(b) Always throw hard and low to prevent the opposition having time to tackle the receiver.

(c) The photographs show two methods of throwing the ball.

DETAILED SEQUENCE OF A LONG GOAL KICK

1. *Long last stride.*
2. *Impact.* Look how far the leg has swung.
3. *Impact.* Look how he kicks through the ball.
4. Follow through. *Now you practise your goal kicks.*

2 Full back play

Over the past ten years full backs have been given more and more licence to attack, but you must remember that the first job of a full back is to *defend*. You must win the ball or be part of the total unit that wins the ball. Only then can you attack.

1. Decide *when* to tackle, and *how* to tackle.

2. Learn *how* to 'contain' your winger (that is, to move close enough to restrict his movements and decisions) and 'jockey' him into a position where you can tackle him.

3. Learn to judge when you can intercept the ball and prevent it from reaching the winger.

4. Learn how to position yourself to cover attacks down the other flank, yet still be able to win the ball if it were changed to your winger.

5. Learn to contain *whoever* comes into your area.

6. Try to clear your lines with a volley kick or a powerful header.

7. You must be on the look-out to support forward, and possibly overlap into advanced positions. When in advanced positions you must accept the responsibilities for crossing the ball (centring it from the wing).

8. Learn to play both short and long passes accurately.

9. Learn to do the simple things consistently well.

10. You need to be quick, tenacious, and skilful.

SUCCESS
Kenny Sansom
(Arsenal and England)
Photo by Bob Thomas

INTERCEPTION

1. Anticipate the pass.
2. Judge speed of ball.
3. Select point of interception.
4. Select surface to make contact with ball.
5. Decide whether to play first time or to control it.
6. Consider the possibilities of who to pass to.

Manny Kaltz (West Germany) moves away with the ball.

Photo by Bob Thomas

JOCKEYING

1. Get close enough to crowd him, and keep his eyes down on the ball.
2. Close in on one side and let him go the other. Always be slightly side on — never square — then you will not be beaten on the turn.

Paul Power (Manchester City) closing in on Glenn Hoddle (Tottenham Hotspur) waiting to tackle.

Photo by Bob Thomas

22

INTERCEPTION

Judge the speed of pass.

As the ball is played wide to No. 10 the white defender attempts to intercept.

(a) If he moves early towards the ball on line 1 he will fail as he is running against the flight of the ball.

(b) If he moves towards the man (line 2) he forces No. 10 to move inside to meet the ball.

(c) He needs to run alongside the shortest line to the flight of the ball marked 3.

JOCKEYING

1. Too far away to influence the player on the ball.

2. Too close — easily beaten.

3. You 'jockey' by closing down on your opponent and keeping at least two or three yards from him.

23

FRONT BLOCK TACKLE

Nicky Reid (Manchester City) makes a firm front block tackle against Ricardo Villa (Tottenham Hotspur).

1. You must decide when to tackle.
2. That is, when you know you can make contact with the ball.
3. Make sure your feet are close together and that you adopt a sitting position and resist initial impact.
4. This sitting position will give you the necessary firm base to lever the ball away from your opponent.

SLIDING TACKLE

1. You make sure that you will overtake the ball as you hit the ground.
2. This will allow you to hook your foot round the ball and drive it through or away from your opponent.
3. Wait, and time the tackle so that the ball cannot be flicked over tackling leg.

Tony Galvin (Tottenham Hotspur) wins a sliding tackle against Ray Ranson (Manchester City) assisted by Glenn Hoddle (also Spurs).

Photos by Bob Thomas

24

WRONG
1. Body and leg straight.
2. Opponent has advantage and wins the tackle.

RIGHT
1. Sitting position. Strong first pressure to clamp the ball against opponent.

2. White defender in a good position to pull the ball over his opponent's foot.

WRONG
Too soon — ball flicked over leg, player runs past him.

RIGHT
1. Good approach to catch opponent and overtake ball.
2. Time tackle to pin ball against opponent's legs. Often repossession is achieved or ball played into touch.

VOLLEYING

1. Get into line of flight.
2. Hit into the flight of the ball.
3. Do not snatch at it or endeavour to hit the ball too early because you will slice it or hit it high into the air.
4. Kick with the instep and hit late in flight to ensure a full leg swing.
5. For short volleys the side of the foot is used, as in this photograph, with the above four factors in mind.

Phil Neal (Liverpool and England).

HEADING

1. Always attack the ball.
2. Only jump off one foot for greater height.
3. Arch the back slightly for maximum power.
4. Hit through the ball and head upwards for distance. You have a whipped motion in the body like a jack-knife.
5. Photograph shows Colin Waldron about to head the ball away. Note the arch of the body.

Terry Butcher (Ipswich) outjumps Tony Woodcock (F.C. Cologne).

Photo by Bob Thomas

26

VOLLEYING

Square onto line of flight. Feet in correct position for contact.

Timing Allow ball to drop low enough for maximum impact.

Direction is in relation to point of impact. Hit through the ball.

Follow through.

POWERFUL DEFENSIVE HEADING

Reverse of arch. Powerful impact on ball.

Good arch, well off ground.

One-footed take off.

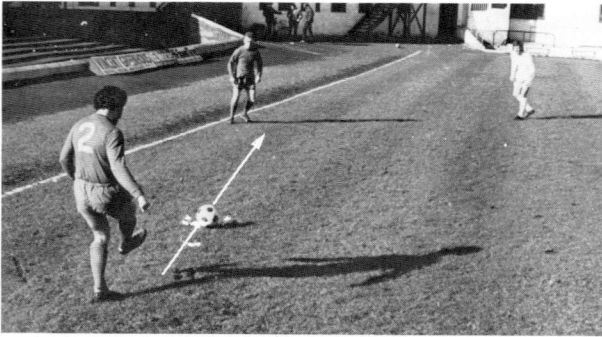

OVERLAPPING
Full back plays the ball down the line and follows the ball.

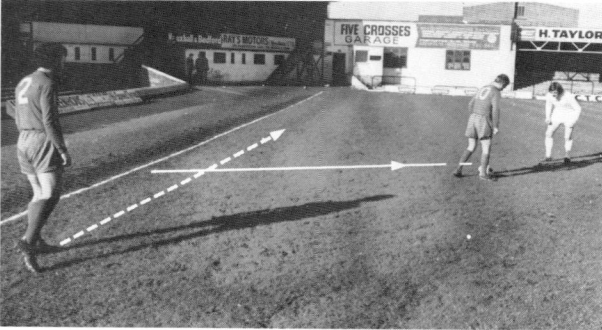

Winger attacks defender, thus creating a channel on the outside.

Pass given too soon.

Pass given too late.

PERFECT
Ball played at the right time to beat the opponent and coincide with full back's overlapping run.

3 Centre back play

My advice to all big, strong boys with ability is: learn to become a competent all-round player and express yourself fully – don't just rely on your covering players.

1. You must learn to head the ball to clear your lines from all angles.

2. You must learn to time your jump so as to give yourself maximum opportunity to win the ball, and you must overcome the physical challenge by getting your chest over the shoulders of your opponent when heading the ball.

3. You must learn to tackle on both sides using either foot.

4. You must try and stop your opponent turning, by marking – that is, shadowing him – very closely.

5. You must learn to turn quickly and be prepared to run with your man when necessary.

6. You must read the intended passes of the opposition and attempt to intercept.

7. When in possession learn to go forward and become a good passer of the ball; don't just be prepared to let colleagues take the ball from you.

8. You can be of great value at corners, throw-ins and free kicks if you become an outstanding header of the ball.

9. You must work instinctively with your goalkeeper to make early decisions on who is to attack the ball. There must be no hesitation.

10. You need to be confident, strong and prepared to use your skill. You should be the most dominant player of the team.

SUCCESS
Phil Thompson (Liverpool and England).
Photo by Bob Thomas

HEADING TO BEAT AN OPPONENT

1. Always attack the ball and jump close to your opponent.

2. Make sure you get a good one-footed take-off.

3. Try and get your chest above his shoulder – this will give you more room to head the ball.

4. Keep your eye on the ball and clear your lines.

Tommy Caton (Manchester City) beats Garth Crooks (Tottenham Hotspur) in a heading duel.

Photo by Bob Thomas

MARKING AN OPPONENT

1. Keep close so that you can dictate to him all that he might do.

2. Do not let him turn.

3. If a player attacks you – move towards his challenge and stop the initial threat to goal and push him sideways. Obviously you mustn't get too close so that he can dribble past you.

4. Most important of all – don't just follow the ball, but turn with your opponent as shown in the sequence on page 33.

John Gidman (Manchester United) marking Kevin Keegan (Southampton).

Photo by Bob Thomas

WRONG: FAILURE

Marking too far away to be able to pick up the flight of the ball.

Head fails to make contact as you duck into opponent.

RIGHT: SUCCESS

Good take-off to attack the ball.

The defender has really stretched towards the ball and is well clear of the opponent to head clear.

MAN TO MAN MARKING

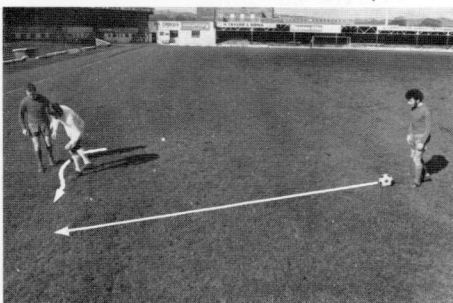

WRONG: FAILURE
1. Player attacks defender.
2. As the ball is laid off, defender turns with the ball.
3. Defender now finds the ball played behind him and can offer no challenge.

RIGHT: SUCCESS
1. Player attacks defender.
2. As the ball is laid off defender turns with his man.
3. As the ball is played through, defender has every chance of winning it.

4 Sweeper or covering centre back play

Priorities

1. You must be well equipped technically, and consistent.

2. You must understand opponents' direction of attack and be aware of their passing possibilities.

3. Never take unnecessary risks, because usually you are the last man.

4. As with all defenders you try to 'intercept', 'jockey' or 'tackle' in that order – but if you read the game well you will intercept the ball frequently.

5. When called to mark man for man you must turn and go with your man as described for the centre back.

6. Your understanding with the other centre back is vital.

Remember:
(a) Never get too close to him when you cover.
(b) Never get caught square with him – as you can then both be beaten by one pass.
(c) To make early decisions as to who will make the first challenge to contain the man on the ball.

7. Your understanding with the goalkeeper is also vital.

Remember:
(a) Because of your line of cover – between ball and the goal – you are liable to take up similar positions to the goalkeeper. Listen to his calls and directions.
(b) On crosses *do not* take balls which the goalkeeper can take. Early calls will help.

8. Do not be afraid to break from the back and move forward. Quite often you are unmarked and you can release players in front of you.

9. You need to be a very good passer of the ball. Practise long lofted passes over players.

10. Again – you must *concentrate totally* and observe all the listed points.

SUCCESS
Alan Hansen (Liverpool and Scotland).

Photo by Bob Thomas

INTERCEPTION

1. You must 'read' the intended pass.

2. Position yourself in order to win it. Be careful not to make a wrong decision and find yourself committed, then miss the ball.

Bryan Robson (West Bromwich Albion and England) leaps forward to intercept against Brazil.

Photos by Bob Thomas

JOCKEYING

1. Stop him turning.

2. Position yourself to intercept.

3. Try to prevent the ball being played past you.

4. You must be close enough to stop the shot.

5. If the ball is laid off then you must retreat far enough to cover the immediate danger.

Mick Mills (Ipswich) keeping a close eye on John Robertson (Nottingham Forest).

COVERING

1. Position yourself so that you can cover your colleague and be able to move in if he is beaten.

2. Try and assess the next pass.

3. Be quick to move in if the man you are covering is beaten or, as in the photograph, to cover back if your colleague is beaten.

4. When covering from a distance, try and fill the space into which they could play.

5. Overall — try to assess when to cover players and when to cover space.

Tommy Caton (Manchester City) covers round behind Ray Ranson (same team) to win the ball.

INTERCEPTION

Ball played in. White defender assesses the speed and line of pass.

Defender attacks the ball, to win.

JOCKEYING

Ball played in.

White defender keeps his body between the ball and the goal.

Defender must be alert to pick up the change of direction.

COVERING

1. White defender too close; both beaten by one pass.

2. White covering defender too far away to assist his beaten colleague.

3. White defender now positions himself to cover his colleague and the space behind.

4. As attacker beats defender 'white' is easily able to move in and tackle.

5 Midfield play: attacking

The creation of the majority of attacks stems from the flair and skill of the midfield players. They say that 'great players are great passers of the ball'.

1. You must learn to understand, when in possession of the ball, the best possibility of passing.

2. You must understand the principles of passing which are:

(a) accuracy – play to feet;
(b) timing – when to play it;
(c) weighting – how hard to play it;
(d) angles – where you can play it.

3. You must be able to screen it and turn.

4. You must be able to control it from all angles and all heights.

5. You must understand your defensive responsibilities of containing and winning the ball (I will deal with these aspects in the next chapter on page 58).

6. You must be prepared to go forward with the ball and run at defending players.

7. You must be able and willing to beat an opponent by dribbling.

8. You must combine with colleagues to get past defenders in possession, with a variety of different types of passes.

9. You must be prepared to strike at goal when you have run into forward positions.

10. You must want to be *involved* all the time. If you continually demand the ball and have the ability to back up these demands with the desire to win, you will become a successful midfield player.

SUCCESS
Gerry Francis (QPR and England).

BALL CONTROL

Move into line of flight of the ball.

Offer correct surface — inside of foot.

Relax and withdraw to control.

Move into line of flight of the ball.

Offer thigh to the ball.

Relax and withdraw to control.

Move into line of flight of the ball.

Offer chest to the ball.

Relax and withdraw the chest to control.

Screening

Reason for screening

(a) When no pass can easily be made.

(b) When an opponent moves in to mark before you can turn and makes it a very tight situation.

How to screen

(a) You must put your body between the opponent and the ball.

(b) You must try and get sideways-on; then you can be playing the ball while being aware of the defender.

(c) Quite often, as the ball arrives you can get sideways-on by attempting to move one way, then quickly moving the other.

Here the defender has a chance of prodding the ball away. He will also be able to tackle as the attacker turns.

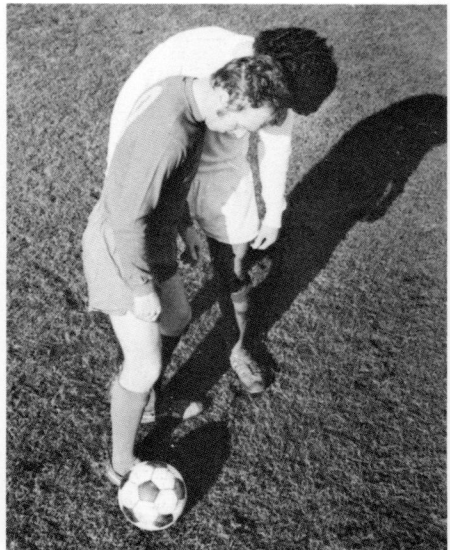

By being sideways-on to a defender you can resist the tackle more easily, and the defender cannot get as close to the ball.

SCREENING

Ball played in. Body kept between ball and opponent.

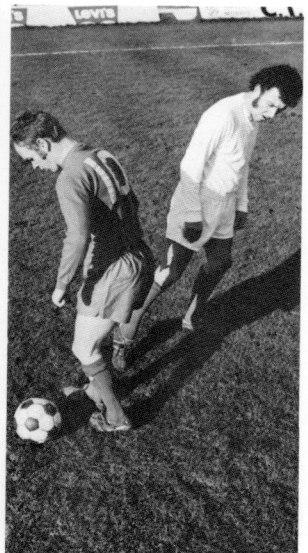

Ball taken and body turned half way.

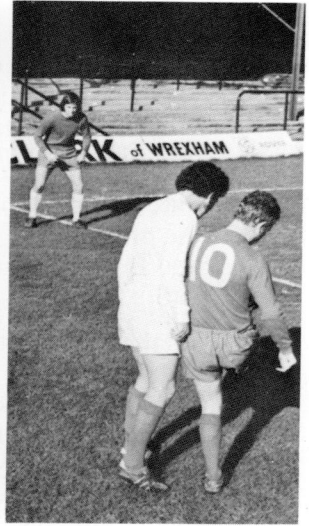

Ball played off. Body still between man and the ball.

Ball played in. Body kept between man and ball.

Ball taken by foot furthest away from challenge.

Spin and accelerate past opponent still keeping the body between the ball and opponent.

Passing

With all groups of players I work with from 8-, 9- and 10-year-olds to senior amateur and professional players, there is one factor I stress that all players should acquire to the best of their skill – *the ability to pass*.

Successful football stems from the total understanding of the principles of passing, the techniques to pass properly and the willingness of colleagues to want to receive the ball.

As the ball moves freely from man to man, each player has to look, control it, screen it if necessary, look again and pass. Sometimes a ball will be played off first time as I will describe later (on page 56). The above sequence is the learning one; if you want to become a good player then you must be able to perform within this sequence.

Here again are the principles of passing:

1. Accuracy
2. Timing
3. Weighting
4. Angles

For a ball to be played off first time – all of these principles must be combined in one movement

If you cannot pass – you cannot play

ACCURACY OF PASS

1. You must play to feet.

2. To keep possession you must be able to play the ball to colleagues at short and long distances.

3. Use inside or outside of foot, as long as the ball reaches its destination.

4. The ability to pass to hit moving targets is vital in the campaign for penetrating behind opponents.

As a colleague moves, the ball must still be played to hit his feet as he arrives in space.

WEIGHTING THE PASS

1. Considerable judgment is required for the pass to beat a defender. This pass is much too hard and runs into touch.

2. This judgment requires high skill in being able to play by 'feeling' the ball and playing it just hard enough.

This shows the ball has been played too softly and the defender has intercepted the pass.

3. In this photograph the playing of the ball at the correct speed has produced the required accuracy of pass by hitting the feet of the colleague as he runs past the defender.

TIMING THE PASS

If you understand the points on accuracy and weighting a pass – now comes the big test. You have to understand *why* you pass and exactly where you pass.

1. You are always trying to get the ball behind defenders. No. 2 plays the ball too soon and the white defender wins it.

2. No. 2 delays his pass and the white defender cuts the angle and denies the pass.

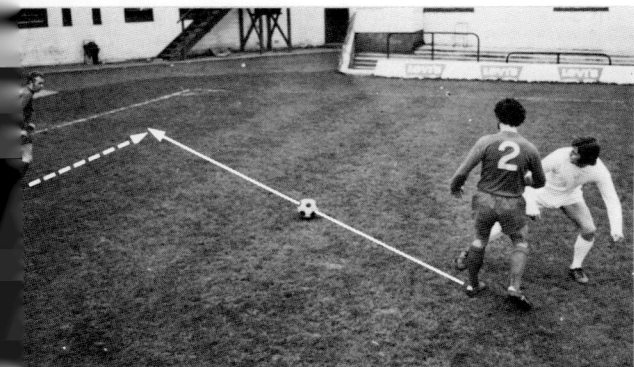

3. The perfect pass is made. The white defender has been attacked, totally committed and beaten by the pass. At that point, with your colleague at the right *angle*, and at the right *time* – the ball is played.

47

LONG THROUGH PASS Not only must you be accurate with short passes, but with those over 30 and 40 yards. Good passes such as the one in the above photograph can go past six defenders and leave the recipient with only one player to beat. Note also the support of white colleagues.

SUCCESS

Trevor Brooking (West Ham and England).

THROUGH BALL

When one side works down a flank, the defence can get drawn towards the ball. This allows players to run from midfield for a through pass. The pass must be played at the right time to coincide with the run of your team-mate and it must be hit hard enough to reach him.

CHANGE OF PLAY

Players are attracted to the ball. The above photograph shows that a quick change of play often puts the full back into space with a chance of playing the ball through early before the defence can re-organise. Two short passes followed by a long pass.

LOFTED THROUGH BALL

Not all passes have a clear route forward, so players need to play lofted aerial balls in order to play over intervening defenders. This photograph shows a long ball played by a centre back to the head of one striker — who flicks on to his colleague. This must be an accurate pass to gain any advantage.

LONG-LOFTED PASS

Remember:

Never try merely to reach your colleague with a long ball — it will always tend to drop short. Always try and hit it over him and the pass will tend to be correct.

Long last stride.

Impact. Note non-kicking foot is slightly away from ball.

52

Impact from side. Look at the speed at which foot hits the ball

Long, well-balanced follow-through.

53

SUCCESS

Asa Hartford (Everton and Scotland).

Brian Flynn (Leeds and Wales).

CHIPPED PASS

Note the speed of the foot as it swings down to strike under the ball.

Note there is no follow-through. Back spin is imparted onto ball as it lifts into the air by the foot. acting as a wedge.

1. It is vital for you to be able to 'chip' the ball. Always be prepared to try it out because there are many occasions when the only way through is over the top of defenders in very cramped space. Practise making the ball spin backwards rather than bouncing on.

2. If the ball is rolling towards you it is easy to stab at the ball to impart a back spin.

3. Obviously it can be of great advantage at free kicks to delicately 'chip' it over the defensive barrier.

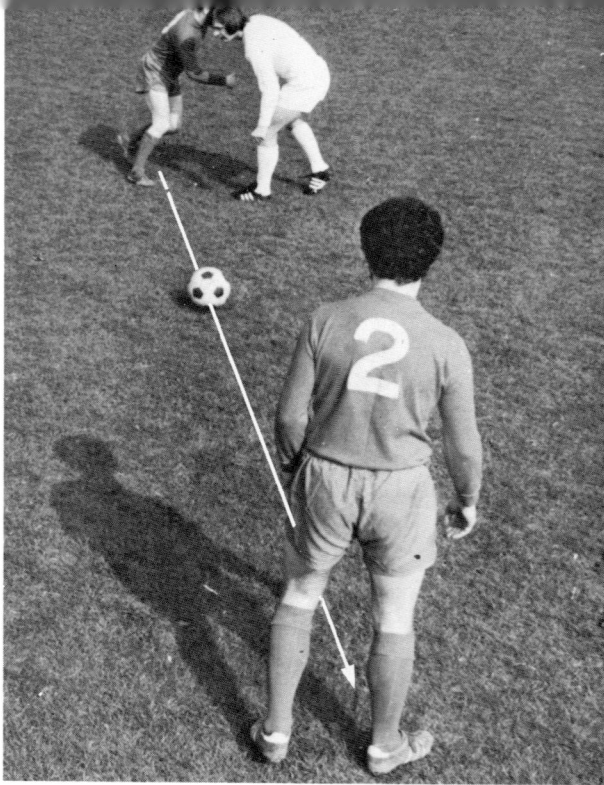

WALL PASS

This refers to a pass that is returned first time. No. 2 acts as a wall. His colleague runs at the white defender and when he is close enough, as shown in the top picture, he plays the ball to No. 2. Then he runs round the far side of the white defender and collects the return pass, as shown in the lower picture.

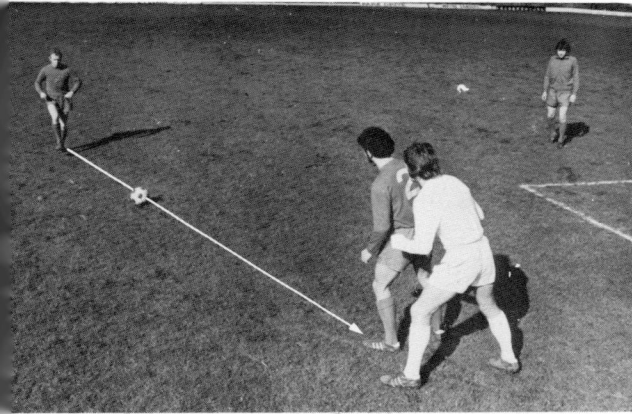

SETTING-UP PASS

This is confusing because it is very similar to a wall pass, but the *timing* is different.

(a) Ball played in.

(b) The ball is not played off first time but the receiver waits and screens the ball until his colleague is in position, then plays it.

or
(c) Having received it he feints to play it back to the server, but, at the last second, turns and plays it to a third player.

6 Midfield play: defending

1. You must continually anticipate the counter-attack.

2. You must work collectively to prevent opponents playing the ball past you.

3. The nearest player challenges the player on the ball.

4. Other players support this challenge.

5. If this initial challenge prevents forward progress then the ball must be played backwards or sideways and can perhaps be swept rapidly to the other side of the field. As defenders you may have to pass opposing players on to colleagues. Never give a player free time on the ball and you will eventually win the ball.

6. You must also be prepared to shadow opponents and run with them until you can easily pass them over to a rear defender.

7. One of the great problems of containing a player, particularly in midfield, in your half of the pitch, is to get close enough to influence your opponent's decision. You must be no further than three or four yards away. If you are further away than this he will be able to make free selections and decisions. This requires you to make an early decision to contain. It also requires you not to get so close that you are easily beaten.

8. As with all defenders you should attempt to intercept, jockey, and tackle in that order.

9. Frequently you have to fill in to the rear of the defence, but don't go in until it is necessary to do so because you clutter up the defence and reduce the efficiency of their decisions.

10. Remember you are like pieces of a jigsaw puzzle. You each have a job to do – but don't try to do everybody's job for them. Midfield players fill the spaces and bind the defence together.

SUCCESS

Terry Yorath (Captain of Vancouver Whitecaps and Wales).

CONTAINING IN MIDFIELD

It is important to deny the opposition time on the ball — time to decide what to do and where to pass. So think and act swiftly. In this photograph a red has made an early challenge and this challenge is supported by two close colleagues. It therefore makes the opposition's passing angles and chances of penetration difficult. Through this principle of 'delay', the opposition are contained in midfield.

Defenders can be really exposed when in possession if tackled early. If forwards move in quickly and contain their rear opponents, they give their midfield colleagues and defenders so much more time to organise themselves and mark tightly. Furthermore if, in this photograph, red 11 takes the ball from the white full back, his path is clear to goal. One factor is important and that is that forwards must not just rush in to tackle because they could be easily beaten.

60

Competition

Games tend to be won by the side that dominates in midfield. You first of all dominate in midfield by marking well enough to stop the other side dictating play. Then you attempt to go forward, and prise open your opponents' defence.

Remember there are certain responsibilities

1. As we said when discussing central defenders, man to man marking is an important skill for midfield players. You must turn and go with your man sometimes over a long distance.

2. Each player has his responsibilities; some are better at winning the ball from opponents than others. Even if you do not tackle well you must carry out the defensive requirements of containing the opposition.

3. You must be careful when going forward in attack and know that if you are caught out someone will fill in to your position behind.

4. You should work as balanced in midfield as at the back of the defence – never be square and always work in relation with your colleagues. In other words share the load with your colleagues, and cover each other. It is surprising how efficient you can become.

5. Whenever you, or any defender, are beaten, you must recover in order to get goal side of the ball.

SUCCESS

Peter Nicholas (Arsenal and Wales).

Photo by Bob Thomas

John Wark (Ipswich and Scotland).

Photo by Bob Thomas

7 Wing play

SUCCESS

*Leighton James
(Swansea and Wales).*

In an age where wingers seem to be unfashionable let me say that any side that plays without wingers or at least with one winger, and one who can operate on a flank, have little chance of playing fluent football. The reason is simple: there is more space on the flanks and this gives players more time to select what to do. It also gives them more time to penetrate their opponents' defence. So good wingers are essential. and here are the main points you must remember.

1. You need to be able to control the ball and turn towards your opponent. Keep your head up and be aware of possibilities of passing.

2. You must be prepared to attack him with the ball and beat him mainly in the final third of the field. This requires certain skill factors: (a) close control;
   (b) change of direction or a feint;
   (c) change of pace.

3. The great problem is to be able to run at speed with the ball, still retain the close control, and watch out for a chance to pass.

4. You must use your body to throw an opponent one way so that you can go the other.

5. The important factor in 4 is that you should get close enough to your opponent that when you have thrown him one way and go the other – *you go past him.*

6. Having gone past him, accelerate away giving him no chance of a second tackle.

7. If you beat him on the inside do not be afraid of going for goal – and shoot.

8. If you go on the outside go for the goal-line and cross the ball into the goal-mouth, aiming at near post or far post.

9. Remember if you take on several defenders – there is no need to try and beat them all as you have created a numerical problem near goal anyway. You could cross the ball straight away.

10. As with any other position on the field, confidence is the key to successful wing play. You must believe in your ability to beat opposing players – and this only comes from a lot of practice.

DRIBBLING

1. You must take on the defender.

2. He is trying to 'jockey' you, therefore you must get in close to him so that:

(a) he is square to you;
(b) he cannot anticipate which way you are going.

Here Kenny Dalglish (Liverpool and Scotland) turns sharply to change direction, beating several defenders.

3. From a point close to the defender try and feint to go one way, taking him with you, then you go the other way.

4. As you go you must accelerate. This means that you attack fast enough to get close, but leave something extra to burst away from the tackle — like Robertson is doing here.

5. Try and keep your head up so that you can assess passing possibilities, after beating your man.

John Robertson (Nottingham Forest) bursts away.

Photo by Bob Thomas

66

CHANGE OF DIRECTION

ATTACK DEFENDER

Get close and get defender square.

As you shift his body weight you move off in the other direction.

CHANGE OF PACE

Feint with the body and play the ball past the defender.

Accelerate past defender and bring ball across to prevent further challenge.

CROSSES

For consistent success in attacking play you need to penetrate down the flanks and send over a stream of crosses. Defenders often just watch the ball and lose their men. When you go for the goal-line try and work round the ball so that you can:

(a) hit hard and low for the near post; or

(b) send lofted balls to the far post; or

(c) turn or spin on the ball and curl it in with the other foot.

If the opposing defenders have moved up to the half-way line, a ball played in early behind them is an advantage.

The top photograph shows Steve Heighway (Liverpool and Eire) about to cross. Note how he has to move round the ball in order to cross.

Kenny Dalglish (Liverpool and Scotland) has burst through and is about to cross under pressure.

CROSSING A BALL FROM THE WING

1. As you go past the defender, play the ball into the middle early, before your opponents have had time to regroup and run back.

or

2. Race for the goal-line and pull the ball back towards the edge of the penalty area. Defenders are running to the line with you and your forwards may be unmarked.

BACK VIEW
Note the lean-away of the body from the ball.

FRONT VIEW
The head gives perfect balance, so does the non-kicking foot.

IMPACT
Perfect balance, allowing the swing of the right leg.

8 Strikers

SUCCESS

Paul Mariner (Ipswich and England).

Photo by Bob Thomas

Pelé has scored 1,000 goals in his career, many of them breathtaking in their skill. Greaves, Charlton, Hurst, Dalglish, Keegan, Francis, Ward, Richards, MacDonald, Toshack, Channon, Pearson – the list is a long one and continues and will continue, because the game revolves about, and thrives upon, goals.

In the 1966 World Cup, England – the winners – had 156 shots at goal in their six games to score 11 goals: one goal per 14 shots. Portugal had 154 shots for 17 goals: one goal per 9 shots. Get the habit of striking at goal, and, if you want to get your shots on target, remember these priorities.

1. The ability to shoot with both feet.

2. The ability and courage to be a good header of the ball.

3. The ability to accept, smoothly and skilfully, the ball hit at you, while resisting the powerful challenge from behind.

4. You have to learn to check and make room enough to turn at least half-way round when receiving a through ball.

5. You have to offer yourself as a passing possibility deep in your opponents' defence – which means continual adjustment.

6. When the ball is on a flank you must judge your run into position at either near or far post.

7. When sharing the striking roles, passing possibilities forward are always maintained. As one striker moves forward, the other moves deep.

8. Games have to be won by you up front. You must always threaten to score and maintain your efforts – chase everything, follow every shot in, take many hard knocks – for the half chance to strike at goal.

9. How to score?

    (a) Never snatch at your shot.

    (b) Always hit the target.

    (c) Generally shoot early – then you maintain your advantage.

10. This is the most rewarding of all positions to play. You must try hard to make yourself outstandingly good in the skills mentioned, and you must be physically fit, too, with the courage, determination and confidence to win.

Success comes from scoring goals and, in offering practical advice to all strikers, I give priority to warning them about shots taken on the ground.

Situations for scoring are frequently offered when only the goalkeeper is there to beat, but goals are missed because:

    (a) the shot is snatched, and pulled wide of the goal;

    (b) the player tries to hit the ball too hard;

    (c) the player takes too long in trying to make sure of his shot.

When the ball is in the air it is a different matter. Then you must think about

    (a) *timing*, so that you can arrive to meet the cross;

    (b) *co-ordination*, to produce best impact on the ball;

    (c) *courage*, to beat defenders to the cross.

Wherever and however you strike, hit the one-yard perimeter down each goal post. To do this you must practise and practise, with both feet and head from all angles – particularly from all points along the front of the penalty area.

Always practise against a goalkeeper so that you learn to judge angles . . . you also learn the kind of difficulties he has!

CONTROL AND SHOOT

All controlling movements must be done so that you can strike the ball at goal before being tackled.

You need be only half a yard past the defender to strike at goal.

Kenny Dalglish (Liverpool and Scotland).

The essentials are:

1. The timing of the run.

2. The direction of the run to come from behind defenders.

3. The space in which contact with the ball is made.

74

FAR POST CHANCES

John Toshack (ex-Liverpool and Wales, now Swansea) scores at the far post.

1. The timing of the run to head the ball. (Always delay this run until you can pick up the flight of the ball.)

2. Never get underneath the ball — if you do you will not be able to jump or get any power in the header.

SUCCESS
Ray Kennedy (Liverpool and England).

SUCCESS
Trevor Francis (Nottingham Forest and England).

Photo by Bob Thomas

SUCCESS
Kevin Keegan (Southampton and England).

SUCCESS
Dynamic duo of Garth Crooks and Steve Archibald of Tottenham Hotspur.

Photo by Bob Thomas

APPLICATION OF BASIC SKILLS

9 Principles of play

You can never be good enough; you just have to go on trying. You must not only acquire the many skills involved in your position – indeed I have not covered every possible aspect, but I have given a lead – you must now apply them to the needs of the team.

The game revolves around opposites. Whether you are in direct opposition with the same opponent or varied opponents, you must be able to produce your skills at the right time.

The secret of good, successful, football is complete understanding of each other. Therefore, you have to learn collectively how to attack and how to defend. You have to learn the strengths and weaknesses of each colleague in your team. To do this effectively you must understand that when you have lost possession of the ball *all* players become defenders and are bound by fundamental *principles of play*. These give you ways of defending as a unit, and denying the opposition the chance to score. It is often said that there are only four ways in which a goal is scored.

1. *Mistakes by defenders.* This is obvious – but is a fact. It is important as well to realise that mistakes can be made just by lack of concentration, or they can be made because of pressure put on to the defenders by the opposing forwards.

2. *Failing to challenge the man on the ball.* How many times do you see defenders retreating from the player on the ball and making a desperate lunge when he nears the edge of the penalty area. Quite often this is too late. He can either play the ball past the defenders, or shoot past them.

3. *Failing to support the challenge.* There is no point in just one defender going out as he will be in danger of being beaten and make your defensive problems greater. By supporting a challenge together, you will really be able to

slow down the attack and make them play the ball sideways – because you will cover the space on both sides of the challenging player.

4. *Failing to shadow runners.* Goals are often scored when a player makes an unexpected run deep into the penalty area. If a player runs 'blind' (so that you don't see him) his chance of scoring is greater. All runners must be seen and tracked down.

If you know how goals can be scored then, if you are on the defending side, the principles of defence help you to counteract them. These principles remain regardless of any system your team may decide to play, and they really counteract fundamental principles of attack. So whenever you are in possession of the ball you – and the whole team – are attackers bound together by principles of attack.

Principles of attack

1. The first principle is *possession.* The side in possession dictates play, and all the skills I have mentioned in Part 1 are related to the time when you are in possession.

2. Coupled with possession is *support.* This allows you to *retain possession* in order to carry out your attacks for a longer period, thus giving you more chance to score.

It is said that in most games the ball is out of play or at rest for around 30 minutes. In an even game each side has 30 minutes on the ball. The rest of the time you are either trying to win the ball back from opponents *or* trying to support and retain possession of it longer. The longer you retain the ball instead of being 30–30 it could become 40–20 and you have twice as long to score.

Try and remember that possession is all-important, then you will not give the ball away unnecessarily, neither will you pass it to an isolated colleague and not support him. The above photograph shows the Wrexham players in white shorts linked together, giving positive support to each other as they move out of defence.

Improvisation. The photograph above shows a player flicking the ball up and shooting on the volley on the turn. A magic moment of improvisation.

All passes that go past opponents towards their goal are penetrating. In any selection of pass you must assess which is the best in relation to penetration. Sometimes, if you play it square, your colleague gets the chance to play a better ball through. Passes played sideways and backwards threaten your opponents' goal least. This ball is played past the defenders — and leads to a goal.

This catches the final moment, when the ball is slid over the line — the ultimate penetration — to score.

PRINCIPLES OF ATTACK : WIDTH

In the modern concept of football we hear that we play without wingers. As a team you must accept that if you play without wingers, *someone* has to move into wide positions. In order to penetrate the opposition defence, we must pull their defenders into positions so as not to over-crowd the centre of the field. Movement into wide positions does produce this. *Remember* — if the ball is on the right wing there is no point in the left winger staying out wide on the line; he could come in to the far post to receive a pass. Thus the whole time we examine the effective width that we need. The top photograph shows the meaning of width in attack, as the ball is passed from the left wing. The middle photograph illustrates the effective width needed. The player on the ball has two passing possibilities, one on each side. The ball is played to beat the defender, and a colleague can then run on and score.

PRINCIPLES OF ATTACK : MOBILITY

If players move up and down the same channels, they are surprisingly easy to mark. But if players change the direction of their runs and sometimes run across the path of a colleague, defenders can be confused. Runs, of course, can be made by defenders moving past forwards or midfield players overlapping from the centre of the field out to the wings. The bottom photograph illustrates this by the movement of players from a cross. The runs to near and far post are clearly marked. The run to the far post was behind the defender.

far

nea

82

PRINCIPLES OF DEFENCE: DELAY

The most important principle of defence is *delay*. This means that you have quickly to prevent the opposition playing the ball forward. This will give you time to reorganise and regroup your defence. So you move forward to pick up the man on the ball. This must be a collective effort, with forwards also involved in trying to stop their opponents — or at least slowing them down. The photograph shows delay by a defender. He prevents the ball being played early and each defender has more time to get close to his opponent.

PRINCIPLES OF DEFENCE: COVER

'Cover' means positioning yourself so that your concentration is divided between the challenge to the man on the ball and the man you are marking. Always cover the opponent's approach to goal. If you are spare and only covering the challenge, do not get too close nor too far away. Always be in a positive position where you can *do* something — not in a position where you will be just too late if you have to challenge. Cover is the defensive principle to counteract width in attack. The photograph shows that as the red defenders race back, the midfield player has moved back to cover. He covers space, also the ball back inside. If his colleague is beaten he can make contact.

84

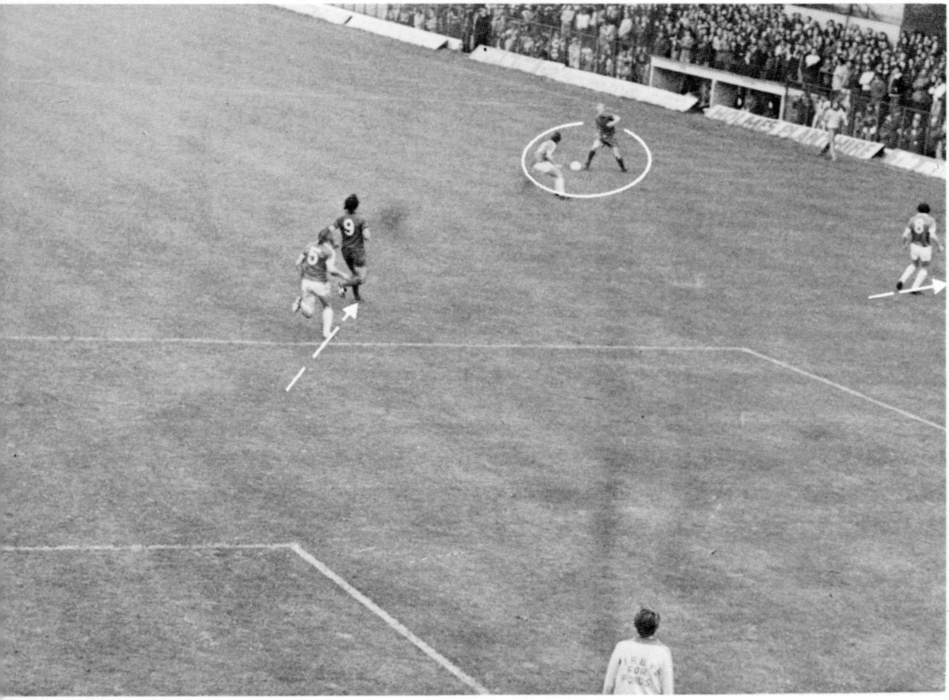

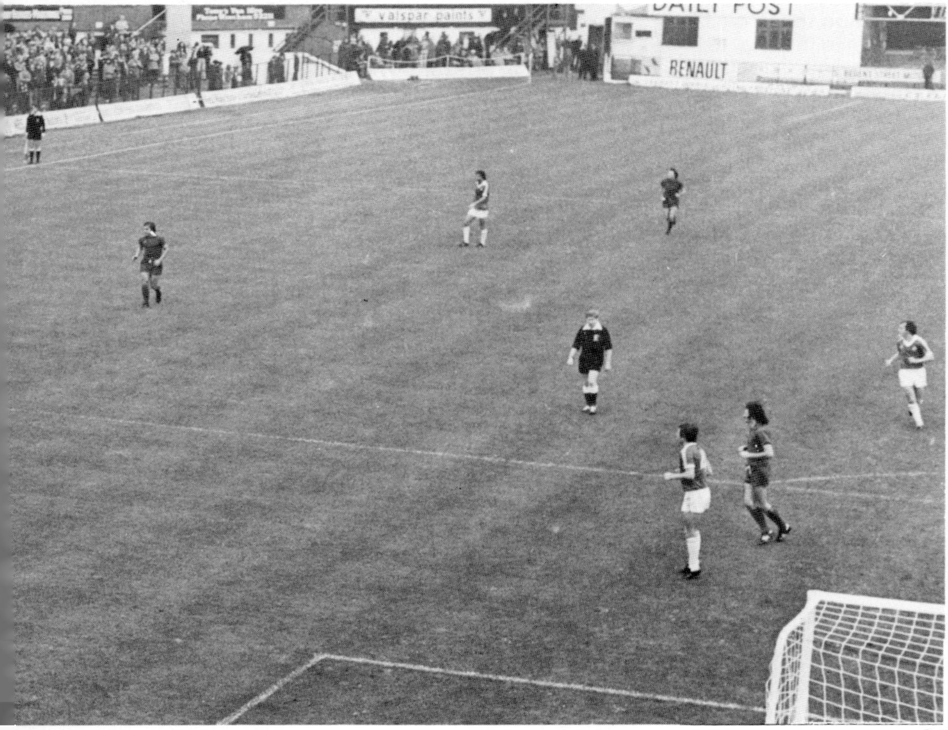
valspar paints
DAILY POST
RENAULT

PRINCIPLES OF DEFENCE: BALANCE

If teams are going to move their players around frequently you must be aware that you may be called upon to fall back into the defence in order to maintain your superiority of numbers. If you and your colleagues *delay* effectively it makes it easier to *cover* and *balance*. Thus, the principles of attack, of *Penetration, Width* and *Mobility*, have definite opposites. *Delay* is the antidote of penetration; *cover* the antidote of width; and *balance*, of mobility. Whatever system you play you constantly work as a team to prevent being outnumbered in any part of the field. Note in the photograph how well spread and how well the Wrexham players (white shorts and socks) are *balanced* to repel this attack by Swindon (dark shorts and socks).

PART 3 *RESTARTS*

10 Corners, Throw-ins and Free Kicks

It is often exciting to be able to plan how to score, or at least strike at goal, from a corner, or throw-in or free kick. These require special skills and must be selected from the abilities within the team. I find that by having set plays worked out, with my players, they are a move ahead of the opposition and get great enjoyment from making the moves work. It also helps in stopping the opposition steal a goal because we are aware of what they might do.

Throw-ins, corners and free kicks are very much dependent on the laws of the game and in all instances you must abide by the referee's decision. Remember that the game has stopped and that the opposition has to wait for you to play to restart the game. You actually dictate the game. At free kicks and corners the opposition must also be 10 yards away from the ball. From corners and *direct* free kicks a goal can be scored direct. From throw-ins and *indirect* free kicks, the ball must touch another player before entering the net for a goal to be scored.

I usually divide the field of play into three. 1. The defensive third: here no risk is taken and safety at all times is the order of the day. 2. The middle third: possession is the most vital factor, because from here we spring-board to attack. And not just the initial possession from the throw is important – *continued possession* is our aim. So from throw-ins we work collectively for a build-up; from free kicks often short quick balls are played to maintain an advantage. 3. The attacking third: here everything is geared to finding ways of striking at goal.

For all restarts in 3. we have to observe certain principles. First we decide which space we want to attack, and secondly we decide how to draw defenders away from that space. Finally we need two skill factors for success: one, a perfect kick or throw, and two, perfect timing to attack the ball in the space to strike. Overall, of course each player has to accept the responsibility of the ball in tight situations.

CORNERS: DEFENSIVE

(Positions before corner is taken.)

Note the rectangle formed by two full backs and two centre backs in the dark shirts to protect the goal-keeper, and the marking of No. 6 inside and in front of the attacker on the goal-line.

Defenders mark closely — goalkeeper attacks the ball and wins it.

An early call by the goal-keeper allowed him to move to attack the ball but he is well covered by the centre half.

CORNERS: TO STRIKE

Defenders box 'round the goalkeeper' to deny any available spaces, therefore the back defenders must be pulled away from the goal. In this photograph three attackers have grouped together deep on the far side of the box and have pulled three defenders away leaving a large central space to attack.

The three attackers have a phased run, one behind the other. The first moves early, followed by the other two, therefore there are three points at which a possible strike can be made — near post, centre goal or the far post. In this photograph the second runner (the centre forward) scores a central goal.

89

The first photograph shows the ball thrown to a tightly-marked forward. It is now up to this player to screen the ball and exploit this one-to-one situation. Note players near the goal awaiting the outcome.

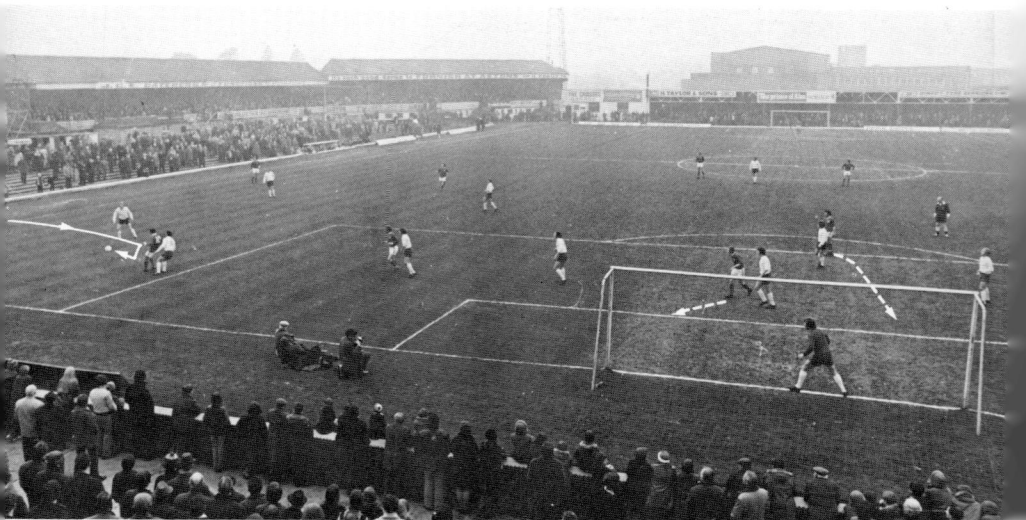

The second photograph from the opposite flank, shows the ball thrown to feet and the ball returned to the thrower. This throw often draws defenders forward and the cross will be played over them to near or far post as the team has previously planned.

INDIRECT FREE KICK

It is vital that all players should get back on to the goal-line and arc round slightly, as shown. The two full backs stay on the line and the goalkeeper places himself in the middle of the remaining eight players. As the kick is taken the goalkeeper hurls himself forward as wide as possible to smother the ball, well supported by the eight who close in fast.

FREE KICKS: DEFENSIVE

Defensive wall of 4 players set up, to cover the near post. The wall is positioned by the striker, who has moved back, the full back and the goalkeeper. Rapid instructions are given by the goalkeeper to the full back who is facing him to line the wall up. I always ask the two full backs to go into the wall, also two midfield players.

This shows the deployment of the team in an emergency. No. 11 cuts the space on one side of the wall and the two other strikers fill the space on the other. All opposing players are marked tightly — the goalkeeper must see the ball. By setting up a wall, a direct shot to the near post is prevented, and the goalkeeper has less to worry about.

Right *Leighton James scores in great style from a penalty shot against England.*

92

FREE KICKS: TO STRIKE

When deciding to strike from a free kick it is important to realise that we attack certain spaces either to the side of the wall or those spaces on each side of the defenders. The first way is a short ball for a colleague to come for a direct strike at goal. Alternatively, as this photograph shows, two wide attackers can run from right to left, calling for the ball, and drawing defenders. The kick is 'chipped' to the far man who heads it back across goal hoping to catch the defenders on the turn in the wrong position. Note how the two attackers have now turned and are ready to attack the ball again.

PENALTIES

1. Always select where you are going to kick the ball.

2. Do not change your mind.

3. Aim for the yard inside either post.

4. Make a good contact on the ball.

YOU AS A PLAYER

11 Fitness

If you are consistently to perform the skills we have looked at, there is a genuine need to be fit. In other words if you as a player make mistakes towards the end of the game, we must ask you whether your mistakes are through lack of skill or lack of fitness.

Fitness for football is different from fitness for any other game. Football fitness is specific to the basic requirements. What do you actually *do* in the game? You run at varying speeds, you walk, you run backwards, you stop, you start, you jump, you fall, you tackle, you collide, you kick the ball, you run with it, you head it, you jockey an opponent, you throw in, and so on. All these are specific to football – but most of them you can reproduce in training. Therefore, training should be a means whereby you copy these movements and repeat them. Each training session is vitally important in preparing the body for all that will be expected of it on the field.

The body must be capable of endurance, it must have strength and it must be mobile. *Endurance* means that you are able to run, on and off, for 90 minutes. So in pre-season go for long runs – they will tone up your legs and develop your breathing. But movements in football are jerky and do not follow a rhythmic pattern, so don't just keep running straight. Try to vary the distances from 5 yards to 50 yards, and get many stops, starts, turns and jumps worked into your running. Whatever you do, try and work flat out for about 30–35 seconds, then rest, because beyond this you will begin to struggle, and lose both performance and speed.

Strength means that you have the ability to overcome resistance without necessarily having momentum behind you. Defenders jumping for a ball often need great strength to move their body weight vertically. Players need strength for starting and stopping, and, of course, in the tackle he who is strongest should win. Strength can be achieved by weight training, a method of using weights to strengthen each muscle group in turn. You work on an overload principle, e.g. small weight – large number of repetitions; heavy weight – small number of repetitions. Weight training exercises can also be incorporated into circuit training to produce the desired effect on a specific part of the body. However, in weight training be very careful and use the weights within safety margins and always work in pairs. Design your work carefully – never just go and snatch at whatever happens to be laid out.

Mobility is expected of you all the time and is closely connected with endurance and strength. In most of your work you move in a vertical way or forwards. By exploring the range of movements of all joints – ankle, knee, hip and pelvis, spine, shoulder, elbow and wrist – you will become more able to collect and control difficult balls which may be on the fringe of your bodily movement.

Remember

Always record your work whether on a timed run or a timed circuit. Try systematically to reduce the rest between sets of repetitions and to increase, gradually, the number of repetitions. You can use the ball extensively in training, but do not use it when you are working at maximum speed output.

Never cheat in training – you will be the only one to suffer because you are deceiving yourself.

Feeling fit gives you a tremendous feeling of confidence and it is a gratifying fact that as your opponents get more tired and weaker you will still be fresh and mobile and feeling stronger and stronger!

12 Conclusion

There can be no satisfactory conclusion to any book on Association Football because there *is* no conclusion. We are continually learning new tactics, new methods, new skills. There is no substitute for skill and to acquire skill needs dedication: never accept a poor standard of play because then you will never fully realise your potential. You must always, always, aim to do better.

Football is a sport, and you must learn to compete fairly. To commit a blatant foul means that at that moment in time you were second best and you cheated by fouling. Always apply yourself to be first to the ball and develop the attitude to win – but not at *all* costs. You have to become consistent as an individual and as a team so that you can reproduce your skills week in, week out.

I always work for three factors that go to producing the correct sportsmanlike attitude within the team. They are:

1. *Discipline*. There is no room for personal battles with opponents because while these are going on other players are dictating the game and you are not contributing.

2. *Concentration*. You must be continually involved. Never let your attention wander. You must constantly check your position because a moment's carelessness will put you wrong. If all players are capable of personal discipline and concentration, this will produce efficiency, both as an individual and as a team.

3. *Efficiency*. With efficiency you can build a consistent unit – without it the team will be riddled by indecision and lack of confidence.

You will always learn most from seeing great players. Watch the top teams – watch the top individual players and observe all you can. But don't be disheartened if your own early efforts are not as spectacular as theirs. Success may come gradually – but it will certainly come if you have dedication to the game, ambition and, again, be willing to work hard and to *go on trying*.